Seashell.

3

Listen to it.

Written by Betsy Franco
Illustrated by Kristin Sorra

Children's Press®
A Division of Scholastic Inc.
New York • Toronto • London • Auckland • Sydney
Mexico City • New Delhi • Hong Kong
Danbury, Connecticut

For Doug
—B. F.

For Papa and Mama
—K. S.

Reading Consultants
Linda Cornwell
Coordinator of School Quality and Professional Improvement
(Indiana State Teachers Association)

Katharine A. Kane
Education Consultant
(Retired, San Diego County Office of Education
and San Diego State University)

Library of Congress Cataloging-in-Publication Data
Franco, Betsy.
    Shells / by Betsy Franco ; illustrated by Kristin Sorra.
        p. cm. — (Rookie reader)
    Summary: Simple rhymes introduce different kinds of shells, from oyster shells
and turtle shells to peanut and pasta shells.
    ISBN 0-516-22012-8 (lib. bdg.)   0-516-27080-X (pbk.)
    [1. Shells—Fiction. 2. Stories in rhyme.] I. Sorra, Kristin, ill. II. Title. III. Series.
PZ8.3.F84765 Sh 2000
[E]—dc21   99-054172

Oyster shell.
Find the surprise.

8

Crab shell.
Where are its eyes?

Snail shell.
Follow its trail.

Turtle shell.
Watch it hide.

Bird's egg shell.

What's inside?

Peanut shell.
Count the nuts.

Pasta shells.
Eat them hot.

Pie shell.
Roll it thin.

Taco shell.

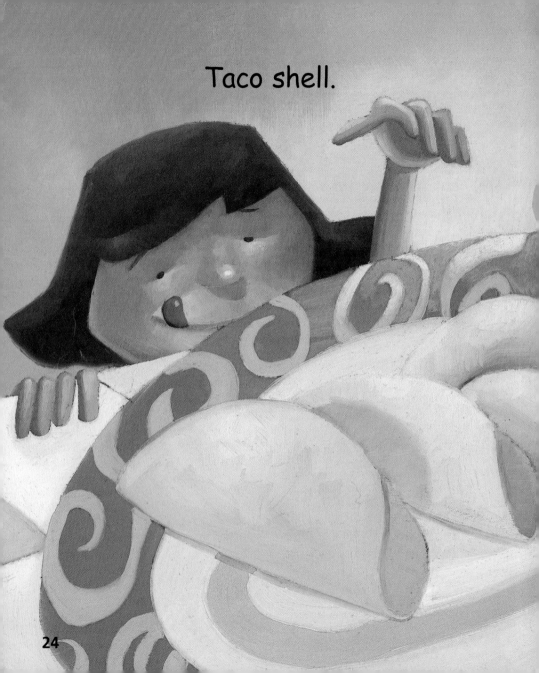

What goes in?

So many shells
for you to find.

Can you count

how many kinds?

Word List (46 words)

are	how	shells
bird's	in	snail
can	inside	so
count	it	surprise
crab	its	taco
eat	kinds	the
egg	listen	them
eyes	many	thin
find	nuts	to
follow	oyster	trail
for	pasta	turtle
goes	peanut	watch
hide	pie	what
hot	roll	what's
	seashell	where
	shell	you

About the Author

Betsy Franco lives in Palo Alto, California, where she has written more than forty books for children—picture books, poetry, and nonfiction. One of her favorite things to do is to play with words, like the word *shells*! Betsy is the only female in her family, which includes her husband Douglas, her three sons, and Lincoln the cat. She starts writing in the wee hours of the morning when everyone but Lincoln is asleep.

About the Illustrator

Kristin Sorra was born and raised in Baltimore, Maryland, and went to New York City to study illustration at Pratt Institute. She recently bought a new home with her husband in Garnerville, New York, where she is now practicing different ways to prepare pasta shells.